To an Iran that honors and embodies Saadi's teachings

Acknowledgements

This book has been a labor of love. It integrates my professional interest in leadership with my culture and it has led me to marvel at the richness and complexity that such integration affords.

I am grateful to my father, Dr. Houchang Nahavandi, who pointed me to Saadi's *Advice to Rulers.* He has guided me through the discovery and reading of Saadi's works and helped me translate and interpret *Advice.* My mother, Mokarram Abrishami, has provided pointed advice and reflection on this manuscript. My husband, Alireza Malekzadeh has offered invaluable help and support in preparing this book and continues to practice its teachings. My daughters Parisa and Arianne have enthusiastically cheered me on during the completion of this book. I hope that they take Saadi's lessons to heart and are able, one day, to visit his mausoleum in Shiraz. I'm thankful to Drs. E.T. Hawks and Anand Desai for their feedback and to Ms. Marisel Herrera who has been a great supporter of this project.

TABLE OF CONTENTS

INTRODUCTION

This book introduces ancient Persian leadership wisdom and advice based on values and principles that have endured for over 3,000 years. While we live in difficult times of economic crisis, regional conflicts, and social change, our challenges pale in comparison to the massive upheaval brought on by Alexander the Great's conquests, the rise of Islam in the Middle East and North Africa, and the Mongol invasion that is among the worst in human history for its cruelty and devastation. The successful leaders who lived and thrived through such times were guided by principles that have been passed down through the ages. These sage principles are based on integrity, kindness, humility, moderation, prudence, consultation, accountability, decisiveness, and astuteness. They are invaluable in helping leaders move their organizations, communities and countries to stability and prosperity and provide guidelines for daily life and relationships to help all of us succeed through day-to-day life and turbulent times.

The wise advice presented in this book is based on the writings of 13th century Persian Sufi philosopher and poet, Shaykh Mosleh-al-din Mushrefuddin Saadi Shirazi, simply known as Saadi to millions around the world. Saadi lived in the tumultuous times following the Mongol invasion of Iran, Asia and parts of Europe. He is known to have wandered a region spanning from Egypt to modern day Iraq and Syria, Saudi Arabia and Turkey for years in search of knowledge, mentors, and patrons. His work is a distillation of his profound and witty observations of the human condition as well as complex spiritual Sufi-inspired reflections. He addresses everyday life with as much wisdom, grace and ease as he speaks to the leaders of the time, urging them towards justice, kindness, humility, moderation and contentment. His teachings are as relevant in today's fast-paced and complex world as they were when he first wrote them in turbulent times of war and change.

Nine Themes and their Significance

Saadi's leadership lessons contain nine key themes with roots in centuries-old literature and philosophy. The themes are:

- Integrity
- Kindness
- Humility
- Moderation
- Prudence
- Consultation

- Accountability
- Decisiveness
- Astuteness

These themes can be traced to Zoroastrian principles dating back to at least 600 B.C. They are reflected in the treatise on leadership written by the 2nd century A.D. Sassanid Leader Ardeshir Babakan, and again found in Ferdowsi's *Shahnameh (Book of Kings)*, the 11th century masterpiece of Persian literature that includes over 100,000 verses of Persian mythology. The leadership themes are further evident in many Persian writings following Saadi. While these leadership principles are in stark contrast with some Western concepts such as Machiavelli's, they are in accordance with Confucius' teachings, the principles presented in the Indian Bhagavad Gita, many ideals found in ancient Greek philosophy, and even in the ideologies of American Transcendentalism.

Saadi's advice to leaders is to face turmoil, adversity and the challenges of governing with unwavering integrity, kindness, humility, moderation, decisiveness and astuteness. His teachings have a strong basis in Sufism with a focus on purity, abstinence, repentance and contentment as the means of achieving closeness to the Divine. Although these underlying spiritual themes permeate his work, the lessons can be applied and practiced in a secular manner as guides to every day life for leaders at all levels.

In addition to providing guidance to leaders, the leadership lessons are significant and noteworthy to modern readers on several grounds:

- First, they have endured many centuries and have influenced the leadership of just, wise and effective rulers who have led vast and culturally diverse empires that were models of peace and prosperity in their times. The themes were developed in times that make our present-day challenges pale in comparison. There is much we can learn from the ancient principles that have guided these leaders.

- Second, the leadership advice presents a unique political philosophy that significantly differs from other leadership approaches that advocate use of fear, ruthlessness, disregard for others, and achieving ends by any means possible. The kinder and gentler Persian approach provides a much-needed alternative to the hardnosed and unfeeling "winner takes all" and "take no prisoner" methods guided by greed and the desire to win at all costs that we observe in some of today's national and organizational leaders.

Third, the ancient Persian leadership principles are akin to many modern leadership theories that advocate integrity-based leadership, authenticity, and connection with followers. They have also influenced the writings of Western thinkers such as the American transcendentalists. In that respect, the ancient lessons have contemporary and Western applicability.

Fourth, the principles apply to leadership at all levels. They were developed to address rulers and monarchs who led vast empires in times of turbulence. However, they provide lessons for day to day life that can guide individuals in leading productive lives in the service of others as well as leaders of organizations big and small. Because Saadi's lessons are as much about living in contentment and treating others with integrity and compassion as they are about leadership, they have applicability at personal and organizational levels.

Fifth, the principles are in stark contrast with the leadership that is currently in place in modern-day Iran and many other countries in the Middle East. The leadership and governance styles practiced in the region are not based on cultural or historical traditions. They do not stem from the political philosophy of the region. If anything, the current regimes and leadership styles are aberrations that go against all ideals of Persian leadership.

Sixth, the principles presented will challenge many Western stereotypical beliefs regarding Iranian culture and leadership. To many around the world, Iran and Iranians appear as extremist, ruthless, cruel, and brutal. The ideals presented in this book show a gentle, gracious and complex culture. These ideals go back for millennia and are a more accurate representation of what Iran and its culture embody. In contrast with their current government, Iranians espouse values that are similar to Saadi's kind and moderate principles.

~~&~~   Finally, in the current climate of conflict and tension with the Middle East, particularly between Iran and the West, knowledge of ancient Persian philosophies can only increase understanding, provide meaningful insight, and maybe point the way to fresh and innovative solutions.

Persia: A Cultural and Historical Primer

Iran, or Persia, as it was known in the West until the beginning of the 20th century is an ancient and rich culture. Vestiges of evolved human civilizations and art can be found in the Iranian plateau dating back to 4,000 B.C. The country presents a documented history going back as far as 3,000 years with the first Persian Empire established in 500 B.C. Although the borders of the country have expanded and shrunk many times and it has weathered many invasions, it has existed as an entity since ancient times and has never been a colony. The rich and long history and territorial and cultural integrity are key factors in how Iranians have viewed and continue to view themselves as a central power in their region.

The first Persian empire was one of the largest and first world powers stretching from modern day Libya and Egypt to parts of India, China, Turkey, and central Asian countries. The empire included a culturally, ethnically, and religiously diverse collection of people. To this day, modern Iran continues to be a gathering of different cultural groups with distinct traditions that have clashed, cooperated and co-existed under a central government. Over the centuries, Persia has been ruled by over twenty-five dynasties, some Persian and some foreign. The last one, the Pahlavi, was toppled by the 1979 Islamic revolution that put an end to the country's centuries-old monarchic tradition. The monarchic identity, characterized by the presence of a powerful central government and symbolized by a king and the cultural elements that accompany such traditions, is an indelible part of Iranian culture and ideals of leadership even under the Islamic Republic.

During its long history, the country has been subject to numerous invasions including those of Alexander the Great in 300 B.C., the Arab invasion of the 7th century A.D. that brought Islam to Iran, and the devastating Mongol invasion of the 13th century. For centuries, Iran has experienced battles between its imperial and Indo-European roots and the cultures of its invaders. What some would consider the true Persian identity has survived through many conflicts, sometimes going underground and resurfacing having integrated new cultural elements from the foreign invaders. The 5th century B.C. Greek historian Herodotus considered Persian openness to other cultures and the ability to borrow cultural elements and make them uniquely Persian to be a defining cultural trait. "Of all men, the Persians especially tend to adopt foreign customs."[1]

Although Iran is at the heart of the Middle East and shares the Islamic religion with its neighbors, its culture and religion are distinct. Persian ethnic roots are those of Indo-European tribes that populated Asia and Europe in pre-historic times. Modern studies of culture and leadership support the cultural distinctness of Iran from its Middle Eastern neighbors. Iran is more accurately grouped with India, Pakistan, and Malaysia than with other Middle-Eastern cultures, which include several Arab countries[2]. The cultural grouping to which Iran belongs tends to be characterized by an emphasis on fairness, altruism, generosity, and caring for others, all factors that are, as the reader will see, essential to Saadi's leadership teachings. Like its Middle-Eastern neighbors, however, Iranian culture values collectivism while it tends to rank in the middle on many of the other dimensions used in cultural studies. The tendency towards moderation, rather than extremes, is, in and of itself, a valued cultural trait in Iran. Research about leadership style in modern Iran indicates that Iranian ideal leadership is characterized by benevolent paternalism whereby the leader is a kind, warm, powerful, accessible,

---

[1] Herodotus. 2007. *The landmark Herodotus.* A new translation by Andrea L. Purvis - Edited by R.B. Strassler. New York: Pantheon Books, p. 73.

[2] R. J., P.J. Hanges, M. Javidan, P.W. Dorfman, and V. Gupta. 2004. *Culture, leadership and organizations: The GLOBE study of 62 societies.* Thousand Oaks, CA: Sage Publications.

and a stern father figure[3]. In comparison, Arab leadership style is often more egalitarian with a strong influence from the Bedouin and Islamic traditions.[4]

In addition to cultural differences between Iran and its many neighbors, the predominant religion in Iran further sets it apart. While the large majority in Arab countries practices Sunni Islam, Iranians are mostly Shiites (or *Shia*). Sunnis and Shiites share a holy book, the Quran, and many principles, but disagree on the succession of leadership following the death of the prophet Mohammad. Sunni Islam relies on a tradition of caliphates where representatives, selected by the faithful, succeed the prophet and rule according to Islamic laws and traditions. Shia Islam believes that Mohammad's descendants and family members are divinely endowed to be the rightful successors to the prophet. It is interesting to point out that while Sunni Islam is, at least in theory, a democratic system of governance, Shia Islam closely follows the Persian monarchic traditions of succession based on progeny.

Modern-day Iran is best known to the West for its Islamic fundamentalism, extremist and ruthless leadership, and relentless

---

[3] Ayman, R., and M.M. Chemers. 1983. Relationship of supervisory behavior ratings to work group effectiveness and subordinate satisfaction among Iranian managers, *Journal of Applied Psychology,* 68, 338-341.

[4] Sarayah, Y.K. 2004. Servant leadership in the Bedouin-Arab culture. *Global Virtue Ethics Review,* 5(3), 58-80; Yousef, D.A. 1998. Predictors of decision-making styles in a non-Western country. *Organization Development Journal,* 19(7), 366.

anti-Western fervor. However, the images of the past thirty-five years must be put in context of several thousand years of history and a culture that is complex and highly diverse, values moderation and, in its majority, welcoming of outsiders and tolerant of other cultures. The sophistication, moderation, hospitality, and openness to other cultures that have characterized Persia throughout history have not simply disappeared as a result of a thirty-five year old extremist regime. These characteristics that are fully reflected in the leadership lessons presented in this book have century-old roots and are not likely to be changed with what can be considered a comparatively small blip in the country's very long history.

A Brief Biography of Saadi

Shaykh Mosleh-al-din Mushrefuddin Saadi Shirazi (1209/1210 – 1283/1291) is a mystic Persian Sunni philosopher and poet who lived in various cities in the Middle East, India, and North Africa during the tumultuous period of the Mongol invasion. He was born in the city of Shiraz in southwestern Iran and was orphaned early in life. He left home to study at Baghdad's famous Al-Nizamiya school where he is reputed to have excelled at his studies. After witnessing the Mongol sack of Baghdad, he was taken into slavery by crusaders in Syria and forced to dig ditches. Saadi travelled for 30 years throughout war-torn and desolate regions, sharing shelter and bread with people from all walks of life, and meeting kings and paupers along the way. He returned home to Shiraz where he found a powerful patron and became one of the city's most celebrated citizens. His most famous writings date to this last period of his life. His mausoleum in Shiraz is a tourist attraction and a place of meditation much cherished by Iranians.

Saadi is extensively read and known for his wisdom, wit, irony, profound observations of the human condition, and the beauty and joy of his prose and poetry. A quote from the Golestan touting the inherent connection among all people, and the importance of compassion in the human experience, graces the entrance of the United Nations Hall of Nations. He is not only beloved by Iranians and other Persian-speaking people, he has also impacted the thinking of writers such as Henry David Thoreau and Ralph Waldo Emerson. Saadi is most renowned for his masterpieces, the *Bustan* (Garden; written in 1257 entirely in verse), the *Golestan* (Garden of Roses; written in 1258 in a combination of prose and verse), and the collection of his lyrics, the *Divan*. His works are widely known throughout the literary world, and translated into many languages. The *Golestan* is one of the first masterpieces of eastern literature translated into French in 1636, German in 1654 and English in 1774. Saadi's writings embody keen observations of the human condition that he acquired throughout his travels. His perceptive and pointed commentary, moral teachings and advice through stories and poems provide the reader with insight into a wide variety of topics ranging from love and youth to old age, education, and governance. He presents a complex combination of awareness of the fragility of life, advocacy for honor, compassion, and social justice, and detachment and disillusionment that sometimes border on cynicism. Throughout, Saadi advocates clear standards of behavior guided by modesty and contentment with little tolerance for sanctimony and affectation.

In addition to broad commentary about the human condition, Saadi has a keen interest in leadership and governance. The *Bustan's* first chapter focuses on "Justice, Counsel, and the Administration of Government" with recommendations for good governance and leadership. He devotes the first chapter of the *Golestan* to the "Conduct of Kings" where he counsels rulers through a series of stories and parables in prose and poetry. His *Ghassideh* or odes, which are lengthy poems in both Persian and Arabic, further provide many leadership lessons. Another of his writings called *Advice to Rulers* (Nasihat-al-molook) is specifically focused on leadership and governance. It offers 151 specific leadership advice and principles related to leading and governing wisely and effectively. *Advice to Rulers* is less known and has not been translated from its original Persian until now. It, along with all of Saadi's writings, presents a clear political philosophy and rich ideals of leadership. Saadi's targets are the kings and princes of his time. He uses examples of fair, just and effective leaders, and stories about evil, corrupt and ineffective ones to counsel those who hold power and exhorts them to be good shepherds of their people. However, his teachings equally apply to daily life and to leading a life of integrity and contentment.

Some License and the Book's Organization

Saadi's prose and poetry are unparalleled. The beauty, subtlety, depth and wit of his writing can best be fully appreciated in the original language. However, many excellent translations of the *Golestan* and *Bustan* authored by literary experts are available[5]. The reader interested in such translations can easily find them.

This book is about **leadership** without any literary claim. It provides advice to leaders at all levels: those leading countries that have responsibility for the life, death and well-being of their citizens, those who lead organizations large and small, and those who are only responsible for themselves or their family. The principles apply

---

[5] *The Golestan of Sa'di: Bilingual English and Persian Edition.* (2008). Translation by W.M. Thackston. Bethesda, MD: Ibex Publishers. Also available online at http://www.iranchamber.com/literature/saadi/books/golestan_saadi.pdf .

The Bustan of Saadi. (2009). Translated by A. Hart Edwards. Los Angeles: Indo-European Publishing. Also available online at http://www.iranchamber.com/literature/saadi/books/bostan_saadi.pdf

equally in all settings and at all levels. I have remained faithful to Saadi's intentions and as close as possible to his language. However, in most cases, I provide an interpretation that is more accessible to the modern reader, rather than a literal translation. I have organized Saadi's guidelines on leadership from the *Bustan,* the *Golestan* and from *Advice to Rulers* into integrated themes rather than following the original order in his writings. Accordingly, I have used "leader" when Saadi referred to ruler, king or master and "followers" for servants or soldiers wherever appropriate. Furthermore, while Persian – or Farsi as it is more commonly known – is not a gendered language, I have used the male pronoun, as was the original intent. The teachings from the *Advice to Rulers* are more direct, prescriptive and less poetic than those found in the *Bustan* and the *Golestan.* The latter are either in verse or poetic and lyrical prose. For all three of Saadi's writings I have relied on the collection of his works edited by Forouqi published in 1997 – 2536 in the Persian Imperial calendar[6]. References to each of his works are indicated with an A (*Advice to Rulers*), B (*Bustan*), or G (*Golestan*). For *Advice* the number refers to actual number of the advice. For the *Bustan* and *Golestan,* the numbers refer to the chapter and poem or story number.

---

[6] Saadi, M. 2536/1977. *Complete works of Saadi* (2nd edition, Edited by M.A. Forouqi), Tehran, Iran: Amir Kabir.

Overall, this interpretation of Saadi's work is faithful to his original intent while introducing his teachings to modern readers to inspire them to approach leadership and their day-to-day life with integrity, compassion, and moderation.

About the Author

Afsaneh Nahavandi is a professor in the School of Public Affairs at Arizona State University where she teaches leadership. She received her PhD in social psychology from the University of Utah with a doctoral dissertation focused on leadership. Her primary areas of specialty are leadership, culture, teams and ethics. She has extensively written about these topics in articles in scholarly journals and chapters, and books. She is the best-selling author of *The Art and Science of Leadership*, now in its 6th edition published by Pearson-Prentice-Hall. Her other books include: *Organizational Behavior: The Person-Organization Fit (1999; Prentice Hall)* and *Organizational Culture in the Management of Mergers* (1993, Quorum Books). She has presented her current work on Persian leadership at national and international conferences, including recently at the conference in Athens, Greece on Leadership and Management in a Changing World: Lessons from Ancient East and West Philosophy. She is a prolific author and speaker and the recipient of several teaching awards at Arizona State University including the 2004 ASU Parents'

Association Professor of the Year Award. She has consulted and conducted leadership workshops for numerous business and public organizations including Honeywell, Valley National Bank, Sea Ray Boats, Phelps Dodge, City of Phoenix, and Maricopa County.

Afsaneh left Iran in 1978 prior to the Islamic revolution and has lived in the U.S. since. She is fluent in Farsi and French with a working knowledge of Spanish.

ANCIENT LEADERSHIP WISDOM

Human beings are members of a whole

In creation of one essence and soul

If one member is afflicted with pain,

Other members uneasy will remain.

If you have no sympathy for human pain,

The name of human you cannot retain.

Saadi's Golestan –

Displayed at the entrance of the United Nations Hall of Nations

Integrity (Dorosti) and
Reputation (Nameh Nik)

"The only thing left in this world is a good reputation."

Integrity is the indispensable characteristic of a leader. Leaders are first and foremost honest. When dealing with followers, they must remain true to their word and, at all times, keep faith with them; they must be authentic. Leaders must act with integrity and guard their reputation. Integrity is a universal concept in leadership. However, its presentation as a key leadership factor in Persian political philosophy is in sharp contrast with other classical writings such as Machiavelli's *The Prince* where deception and treachery are recommended as a means of achieving and retaining power. For Saadi, the leader's good name and success are based on honesty, respect for others, and maintenance of an impeccable reputation which is the primary source of power for any leader. Furthermore, leaders are responsible and accountable for their advisors' and followers' actions. If they surround themselves with dishonest people or tolerate lack of integrity in their followers, they themselves will lose legitimacy and will not be able to lead effectively. Leaders must therefore demonstrate integrity in their actions, role-model honesty, and guard their reputation at all times.

The only thing left in this world is a good reputation. Misery comes to one who does not even leave that to posterity. (A:111)

You can only punish others for corruption when you yourself are not corrupt and are beyond reproach. (A:34)

When the leader is in power, he must act in ways that do not bring shame to him when he leaves. (A:142)

If the leader eats an apple from a subordinate's garden, his followers will rip up the trees by the root. For every five eggs the leader allows to be taken unjustly, his followers will put a thousand chickens on spits. (G:1-19)

- The leader must not support evildoers or corrupt people. The leader who helps such people associates himself with their sins and deserves punishment. (A:14)

- There are two types of thieves: The armed highway robbers and those in the markets who commit financial misdeeds. Both must be dealt with severely. (A:28)

- Do not let your friends intercede on behalf of thieves and criminals. (A:27)

- The leader must keep his dignity and not commit sins or other forbidden acts. He must act and speak with dignity in front of men of knowledge and science and influence. (A:20)

❧ Do not get angry with those who speak ill of you. Why should you not behave in ways that lead them to only speak well of you? When you are unfair, do not expect a good reputation (A:138)

❧ Do not touch people's inheritance, especially orphans'. Such act is unworthy of a leader and will bring him misfortune. (A:110)

❧ The leader must not hide or eliminate the work of those who came before him if he wants his own deeds and work to be remembered and honored. (A:9)

❧ You must not associate with or befriend people who have bad reputations and no virtue because they will influence you. You then will not have the credibility to punish others who commit bad deeds or have no virtue. (A:25)

A good man dies and his reputation survives. (A:119)

A leader who does not treat his people well and expects a good reputation is like a farmer who sows oats and hopes to reap wheat. (A:113)

Make sure that people speak well of you in your absence. Because if they speak well in your presence, it is from fear or for gain. (A:129)

If you desire a good name, hold merchants and travelers in high esteem; they will carry your reputation throughout the world. (B:1-2)

While you are alive, do your best in action, advice, attitude and kindness. When you die, there is no difference between a leader and a beggar. (A:130)

Saadi's emphasis on integrity and the importance of a good reputation are not unique to Persian philosophy. Having integrity is the sine qua non of leadership. This principle extends to all cultures and all situations. Modern leadership research has shown that integrity is a universal component of leadership. People all over the world consider their leaders' integrity to be essential. Acting honestly and with honor is a simple choice leaders must make. Such a choice builds leaders' credibility, another indispensable component of leadership. Saadi puts particular emphasis on guarding one's reputation through one's own actions. He further emphasizes the importance of selecting advisors and friends who act honorably. Leaders can not only lose credibility through their own misdeeds, but also through associating with people who are corrupt. Establishing and then guarding their good name and reputation are life-long pursuits for leaders and according to Saadi, one of the few things that leaders leave for posterity.

Kindness (Mehrabani)

"A cruel person cannot be a leader, as a wolf cannot be a shepherd."

If integrity is the basis of leadership, its cornerstone is kindness. The ideal leader is kind, benevolent and compassionate to all regardless of their station in life. The leader's first and foremost duty is that of a caring father figure who advocates for followers and for those who are too weak and powerless and cannot advocate for themselves. Leaders must attend to their followers' needs to assure their wellbeing and, as a result, reinforce their power and support their own success. Taking advantage of the powerless and weak is a fault and is frowned upon. When leaders mistreat their followers, they hurt themselves. Cruelty and malice are anathema to leadership and considered to be fundamental flaws. Being cruel to followers and even to enemies will bring misfortune to the leader.

Along with being kind, leaders must show compassion, forgive those who stray or make mistakes and show clemency whenever warranted. The duty of leaders, by virtue of the power and privilege they are given, is to treat followers fairly and impartially and assure that justice is done for the powerful and the powerless alike. Leaders are required to right wrongs, pursue justice for all, and demonstrate fairness and impartiality in their decisions and actions. It is unworthy of a leader to be unjust and take advantage of people without power.

Leaders must be kind and compassionate for two reasons. First, these traits are inherent to leadership. Leaders are benevolent father figures. Saadi repeatedly suggests that kindness is the source of power for leaders, either directly or because the leader's kindness and compassion make the country stronger and less vulnerable to attacks. Kindness and compassion serve a second purpose of protecting leaders against destiny. One's actions affect one's destiny, and therefore, they must be carefully thought-out. Leaders' kindness will pay off when they are in need either to defend their position and kingdom, or in the after-life. The recurring themes of goodness for goodness sake along with threat of punishment and retribution provide strong incentives for leaders to act kindly and compassionately.

 A cruel person cannot be a leader, as a wolf cannot be a shepherd. A leader who lays a foundation of cruelty jeopardizes the stability of his country. (G:1-6)

🙰 The leader who protects the weak, protects the country and the state. (A:1)

🙰 You who have the upper hand and can torment your underlings, how long do you think this market will be brisk? Of what use to you is world rule? It would be better for you to die than to torment people. (G:1-11)

🙰 The leader must protect and help the old, the weak, widows, orphans, the needy and strangers. (A:12)

🙰 Do not take the cries and wounds of the poor lightly. One flame can put fire to a city. (A:100)

🙰 The rich and mighty only get respect if they serve and provide comfort to others. Otherwise, they are not deserving of wealth and power. (A: 92)

When your followers get weak and old, don't forget your obligations to them. Even, if old age prevents them from serving you, your obligation to be generous to them remains. (B:1-2)

Leaders are fathers to orphans. They must take care of them better than their own father would, because a leader who is a father must be better than a regular father. (A:13)

Don't turn away the poor from your door empty handed, in case you should wander to the door of strangers yourself. (B:2-1)

Don't oppress the people of this world in case their prayers rise up to heaven (G:1-26)

❧ A wise and perceptive leader does not antagonize or annoy his subordinates. When faced with an external enemy, he will not have to fight on two fronts. (A:63)

❧ It is befitting of those who have power to give to the weak. Greatness demands that one does not touch other peoples' possessions. (A:120)

❧ The leader must support the family and children of the soldiers who die in battle. (A:68)

❧ You who sleep a peaceful sleep, remember that others are awake. You who have power to walk, let the weaker ones accompany you. You with financial means, take care of the poor. Have you seen what the ancient ones have done? Those who were unjust and mistreated the weak have only left a bad name and will pay in the next world. In truth, it is better to be poor and in good health with a good conscience, than to be a leader with all the privileges and a bad conscience. (A:124)

As far as you are able, do not hurt anyone, for there are many hazards in this path. Help out the indigent, because you too may be in need some day. (G:1-35)

Tell the guardians of the frontiers to treat strangers well and welcome them. It affects the safety of the nation. (A:64)

The leader must help those who have been robbed, those whose ships have sunk, and those who have been subject to major tragedies. You must do what you can; it is a duty. (A:43)

The leader must take care of his followers even if it is difficult to do so. Followers may have problems that need to be heard. If possible, the leader must know the wishes and wants of all. A leader who is isolated and angry does not deserve to lead. (A:57)

Be pleasant whenever possible with subordinates and strangers, with family members, with common people, the powerful, and others. Be humble in your relationships. This will not hurt your power; instead, it will make you popular. (A:69)

Every good fortune requires a grace. For wealth, it is charity; for having the power of a leader, it is the protection of followers and assuring their well-being; for being in the leader's entourage, it is preservation of other's possessions; for happiness, it is caring for the less fortunate; for power, it is helping the poor. (A:94)

A leader cherishes and respects all his subjects. (A:136)

The guilty must be punished for his crime. If he provides a service later, he deserves the same clemency as an innocent prisoner. (A:46)

Be mindful of your superior; be kind to your inferiors. (A:148)

Serve those who have been through disasters. They will serve you well afterwards because they have known misery. They can become excellent defenders of the public good. (A:47)

If you have to jail powerful people, treat them with respect, assuring proper nutrition, an appropriate environment and even distractions. Misfortune could happen to anyone. (A:71)

❧ Do not be harsh when you can be kind and courteous. (A:147)

❧ If you punish and fire underlings for a bad mistake, take into account their prior service. (A:65)

❧ Take the cotton out of your ear and give justice to the people. If you do not, the day of reckoning will come. (G:1-10)

❧ It is unworthy of a leader to act unjustly. And when he has to hand out justice, he must remain moderate. If not, he will be the one who commits an offense and there will be grounds for people to complain. (A:35)

❧ A just government is like an unshakable wall. When government acts on whims, cracks appear in the wall. (A:75)

∿ The leader must provide justice and protect victims so that people who are evil and arrogant do not build unjustified pride and are stopped. (A:32)

∿ The leader must hear judicial complaints in person because those around him and security chiefs do not always tell him all that he needs to know. (A:118)

∿ You must not accept any witness without assuring that the person is virtuous and tells the truth. You must not assign punishment without having proven and established the facts. (A:26)

Kindness, compassion and fairness are as essential to leadership as integrity. Taking care of followers is the primary duty of leaders. Saadi advocates a kind and gentle form of leadership where leaders treat followers with benevolence and empathy as a father or mother would. They also must show compassion and generosity and forgive mistakes. Those who make mistakes must be given the chance to change and correct them. Leaders must be fair and just with followers. Much like integrity, acting justly is a choice leaders must make. Taking care of those who have power is easy; the real challenge for leaders is to give voice to the voiceless and assure that they are treated with equity. These concepts are not typically associated with leadership. Instead, leaders often focus on getting things done, sometimes at the expense of their followers. However, leaders must remember that without their followers, nothing can get done. It is the courage and sacrifice of soldiers that win battles; it is the creativity and hard work of employees that turn companies around; it is the dedication and concern of citizens that make a community prosper.

Humility (Forootani)

"Sheep do not exist for the shepherd. It is the shepherd who exists for serving the sheep."

Humility is an essential leadership characteristic. The ideal leader is a humble servant to those he leads, not a superior and overconfident overlord. Leaders and followers are part of an integral whole rather than separate parts. One cannot survive without the other. Leaders must understand that they are privileged to have the opportunity to serve others and they should be grateful for that opportunity and use it for the public good. They must remain accessible and remember that their duty and the purpose of their power and privilege are to serve others. Power and glory must be used to help followers, not for the benefit of the leader. Saadi's Sufism is most evident in this area; leaders, as do all people, must be aware of their own mortality and insignificance and avoid haughtiness and self-importance. Arrogance and hubris are undesirable and likely to cause the fall of leaders. Leaders must do what is right without expectations for recognition. Their good deeds and accomplishments will speak for themselves – as will their mistakes.

A leader is a shepherd for his followers even if he intimidates them with his splendor. Sheep do not exist for the shepherd. It is the shepherd who exists for serving the sheep. (G1:28)

If you want to attain dignity, let humility be your path. (B:4-13)

The leader must never forget the transfer of power from one person to another so that he does not get too attached to his power. He must remember that power and its privileges are temporary. Vanity must not dominate a leader. (A:3)

The leaders are the head; the subjects are the body. What ignorant head tears its own body? (A:53)

❧ The duty of the leader is to serve his followers. Greatness is to recognize and express gratitude to followers without expecting anything in return. (A:89)

❧ You think that you are full of knowledge? How can a vessel that is full receive any more? Rid yourself of pretensions, so that you may be filled. If you are full of vanity, you will go empty. (B:4-12)

❧ Leaders must devote themselves to the service of followers. Serving the poor and protecting the weak strengthen the leader. (A:6)

❧ The leader who does not serve others and does not help them does not deserve to lead and have the benefits of good fortune. (A:12)

The shepherd should not sleep while the wolf is in among the sheep. Protect the needy because a king wears his crown for the sake of his subjects. The people are the root and the king is the tree; and the tree gains strength from the root. (B-1:1)

If a man has talent and skills, they will be obvious to others. He does not need to flaunt them. (A:7)

The leader must be responsible for his old followers and not ask anything in return. Their prayers and gratitude will be worth more than their service. (A: 8)

You hold the place that belonged to someone else before you and someone else before that. You are only a stepping-stone. Do not lose your head. (A:116)

The intelligent leader must serve everyone in accordance to his merits. He must not grant all that is asked because that will deplete resources and will never end. Virtuous people ask for nothing and do not expect to get favors. The interest of the leader is to satisfy those who have virtue and dignity and those who do not demand anything in return, and to serve the most possible. A person with dignity does not ask for anything and the one who asks once will always demand more. (A:7)

The royal treasury is not for the king alone – it is filled for the sake of the army, not for the purchase of ornaments and jewelry. (B:1-4)

Fairness demands that you notice others' good deeds and that you be grateful and that you not forget them. Leaders deserve to lead and have power only because of their subjects. What is a leader without followers? They therefore, must protect followers and if they don't, if they do not serve them, they do not deserve any respect or to lead. (A:97)

If a man has any merit, it will speak for itself. (B:7-4)

You who amass riches in order to have power, be charitable and humble. The real power is the love and gratitude of your people. (A:114)

When you have the purest musk, claim not to possess it. If you have it, it will make itself known by its perfume. (B:7-4)

The bones of the dead talk. If you are smart, you will listen to them and hear their message. They will tell you: "I was like you; I did not value my life. I did not appreciate it and where am I now?" You must not go through life without being useful, without serving others. The leader must take advantage of the time he has. (A:125)

The leader must study the story of the life of ancient and previous leaders. This has several purposes: learning from those who have done good deeds; observing the challenges and failures of the past so they can be avoided; and finally, not losing one's head and not becoming arrogant with power, fortune, and beautiful possessions. All shall pass. (A:21)

Be aware that while you hold good things in your hand, fortune and power move from hand to hand. (G:1-28)

Do not go down a well with the rope of praise. Be deaf and listen to the words of those who slander you. (B:4-15)

Saadi's ideal leader is one without pride or arrogance, one who is humble and a servant to his or her followers. The idea of servant leadership is part of most religious traditions and has been recognized in modern leadership theory and research. The leaders are there for the followers; not the other way around. Remaining humble is a challenge for leaders as power and its privileges can be intoxicating and corrupting. Saadi reminds leaders that they are but one element of a vast universe and that they only have any significance when they contribute to the welfare and wellbeing of their followers and subjects. The lesson of humility is a challenging one for many national and organizational leaders who let power go to their head and assume that others –citizens of the state or employees – exist only to serve and glorify them.

Moderation (Miyaneh Ravi)

"Avoid quick anger. You can kill a living being; but you can't resuscitate the dead. If you break a precious gem, you cannot restore it."

Effective leaders follow a path of moderation, shunning extremes at every opportunity. They carefully and patiently weigh all sides and avoid extravagant and excessive decisions and actions that can cause irreparable harm. Saadi recommends everything in moderation, whether it is games and political maneuvering, or even virtue and prayer. Shunning the extremes or seeking the Golden Mean is a concept familiar to both ancient Chinese and Greek philosophies. Bluster and pretentiousness are bound to lead to failure and should be avoided at all costs. Anything that is carried to its extreme, even courage, kindness and generosity, can have adverse consequences. The middle road is the path to success.

✺ Avoid quick anger. You can kill a living being; but you can't resuscitate the dead. If you break a precious gem, you can't restore it. (A:108)

✺ You can only govern through moderation. (A:79)

✺ Courage is not to attack without discernment and out of anger, it is to control that anger and act with fairness. (A:109)

✺ Generosity is a desirable quality, but not to the point of weakening the state. You must be thrifty with public funds, but not to the point of creating hardship for people. (A:17)

✺ You must not try to achieve immediately everything that you want to do for the country. You must first reflect, then consult others, then act if the majority of those whose opinions are sought approve. (A:30)

Virtue and prayer are desirable. But not to the point of making life bitter and hard for oneself and others. Pleasures and distractions are necessary, but not to the point of making one forget duties towards god and service to others. (A:19)

You must act with care and patience in everything, except when there is immediate danger such as when saving drowning men or putting out a fire. (A:78)

The leader must be as generous as possible, unless the income cannot support expenses. Miserliness is as bad as extravagance; take a middle course between the two. (A:15)

The anger and the authority of leaders must be commensurate with their work and the services they render, but not to the point of making them unbearable and hateful to the population. Games and political one-upmanship are necessary to leadership, but not to the point of making the leader look weak or weak of mind. (A:18)

❧ Kindness has its place in leadership, but it must not be the dominant factor or used as a means of attracting followers. Those who seek a good reputation must be aware that there will always be ungrateful people. If you forget this, you will be accused of weakness rather than given credit for your kindness. (A:16)

❧ Wise men do not think that someone who picks a fight with a raging elephant is manly. The one who is manly does not speak nonsense when he is angered. (G:1-34)

❧ Wealth has a great power: it turns enemies into friends. Amassing a useless fortune turns friends into enemies. (A:112)

> ❧ Eat only when you are very hungry. Speak only when you have something important to say. Go to bed only when you are really tired. Make love only when desire is very high. (A:140)

Saadi advocates moderation in every action. Extremes are dangerous and should be avoided. Although he was a pious and spiritual man, he observes that even religion in the extreme is detrimental. All the desirable characteristics of leaders must be practiced in moderation. Saadi shows a distinct dislike of pretension and sanctimony that often accompany taking behaviors to the extreme.   Leaders must demonstrate restraint and self-control and carefully weigh their options before making decisions. Impetuousness and rushing into action can only create problems. The tendency for moderation is a deeply ingrained Persian cultural trait that may be in contrast with other cultures' tendencies towards high risk-taking. Given the crucial role of leaders and their responsibility for their followers' wellbeing, moderation and shunning impetuousness are wise advice.

Afsaneh Nahavandi

Prudence (Ehtyat – Door bini)

"Be vigilant as if the enemy is at your door. You will not be surprised if he happens to suddenly enter."

Along with seeking moderation, leaders must be prudent, patient and vigilant in their words and actions. They must carefully monitor their own behavior, be wary of strangers and even be cautious with friends. Saadi makes a particular case for silence and discretion. As with other things, leaders must be careful with their speech and the information they share. They must seek solutions that integrate wisdom, kindness, and a long-term perspective that takes into account consequences of their own and others' actions. Haste is detrimental; every action and potential reaction must be weighed and considered before a final decision is made. Just because leaders are kind and compassionate does not mean that they are gullible and have an unrealistically optimistic view of the world. On the contrary, good leaders are aware that they may have enemies and therefore must be watchful to assure their own and their followers' wellbeing. They must expect and demand the best from themselves and others, but prepare for the worse.

Be vigilant as if the enemy is at your door. You will not be surprised if he happens to suddenly enter. (A:149)

 A leader must always think about the strength of his government. He must predict in advance world events. (A:3)

 Beasts are silent and human beings can speak. Those who speak pointlessly are worse than beasts. (B:7-3)

 Do not trust newcomers too much. (A:105)

 Do not slander anyone in front of a wall – often, there are listening ears behind it. (B:7-1)

❧ Do not tell all your secrets to your friends. Friendship is not eternal. (A:55)

❧ One who talks little has a high reputation. Silence is dignity and the concealer of blemishes. (B7:3)

❧ One who defames another reveals his own faults (B:7-5)

❧ Those who speak ill of others in front of you will speak ill of you to others; avoid them. (A:84)

❧ If you don't want a secret to be known, don't tell either your best friends or even your most ardent supporters. Because best friends also have best friends and ardent supporters have ardent supporters. (A:54)

∿ The weakness of a leader comes from not paying attention to his weak enemies or giving too much power to ones who can hurt him. (A:87)

∿ War is only allowed when there are no other solutions. It is better to retreat when one cannot hope to win. One does not fight with the hilt of a sword. (A:90)

∿ Fear the weak enemy because when he is weak, he plots and will fight to the death. The cat facing a lion is weak and he knows it; he therefore attacks the eyes to blind him. (A:127)

∿ You must be friendly to the strong and the weak and sow the seeds of friendship everywhere. You cannot count on the closeness and protection of powerful people and assume that no one can harm you. If someone kills you and your protector takes revenge, you still cannot be revived. (A:128)

Ideal leaders not only take moderate action, they are also prudent and cautious in their decision-making and in their own conduct. The kind and generous leader is not a dupe; he or she is perceptive and prepares for the worse. A highly practical advice from Saadi is the importance of discretion and silence. He recommends discretion in speech and actions. Since leaders are role models and the center of attention, they must be particularly careful about their speech and actions.

Consultation (Mashverat) and

Seeking Knowledge (Danesh Amoozi; Kheradmandi)

"Cherish and respect the men of science and religion and put them ahead of others. The leader must consult them on how to govern"

Consulting experts and seeking knowledge and wisdom must be the focus of everyone's life, but it is particularly important for leaders. Wise leaders pursue knowledge and seek understanding and wisdom. They rely on help from those who have experience and expertise. While leaders ought to be decisive and take responsibility for their followers, they must not be so arrogant as to believe they have all the knowledge and therefore they must seek the counsel of experts. Ideal leaders are wise and knowledgeable but humble enough to know their limits. Leaders' power and positions do not exempt them from needing help and advice from others. Relying on experts with experience is a necessary part of leadership. Consultation is the key to a leader's success, as is having the foresight to know whom to consult.

Cherish and respect the men of science and religion and put them ahead of others. The leader must consult them on how to govern. (A:4)

If you want your father's inheritance, acquire your father's knowledge, because your father's wealth can be spent in a day. (G:7-3)

Never trust big decisions to people without experience. They will fail. (A:24)

Do not trust someone that you have not seen in action many times. (A:150)

Those who are in leadership must seek help from wise men who have a good reputation, integrity, good intentions, come from good stock, have know-how and skills. Those people can dedicate themselves wholly to their work and make people happy. (A:10)

~๖ Advice and moderation come from old wise men who know the world. Strength and war are for young people who lack judgment. (A:31)

~๖ A bag of silver and gold is emptied; the purse of an artisan remains full. (B:7-16)

~๖ Give responsibility to someone who has proven himself; otherwise, you will only get empty promises. (A:106)

Saadi's respect for knowledge, wisdom and experience is evident in all his writings. Science and learning are primary to his teachings. His ideal leaders promote science and the arts and value the insight and wisdom that come from experience. From a practical point of view, Saadi is in agreement with modern leadership research that recommends consulting experts, especially when problems are complex. For Saadi, relying on others' wisdom is an absolute necessity. Even with considerable power, Saadi's ideal leaders do not have to act alone. They must rely on the advice and support of knowledgeable and carefully selected advisors. Saadi's emphasis on the importance of experience is in line with other Asian philosophies where experience is valued over youth and spontaneity.

Accountability (Passokhgooi)

"No oppressor lasts forever, but the curses upon him will last eternally."

The leaders' power and authority and its privileges come with considerable responsibility towards followers and accountability for their actions. Leaders are not only accountable to their followers, as they are their servants, they are more importantly, accountable to a higher authority. Their good deeds will be rewarded and their transgressions punished, if not in the present, but certainly in the future and in the afterlife. This sense of "karma" is present in much of Eastern philosophy and is a foundation of Saadi's teachings. Leaders must do well because that is what good leaders do. However, if that principle is not reason enough for good deeds, leaders must act well because they are accountable to a higher authority. This sense of fate and destiny should convince leaders to act in good faith and serve their followers to the best of their ability. Their actions and their treatment of others matter and they are held accountable for their good – and their bad – deeds.

No oppressor lasts forever, but the curses upon him will last eternally. (G:1-20)

Don't oppress the people of the world in case a prayer rise up to heaven. Make peace with your underlings and be secure from battle with opponents, because followers are a fair leader's army. (G:1-6)

The leader is the leader of his subjects. If he makes them suffer; they will become the enemies of their own kingdom. (A:53)

When the weak gain courage and fight, they deliver blows more serious than the sword of powerful men. (A:121)

Eternity passes like the wind over the desert; bitterness, pleasure, ugliness and beauty all pass. The thoughts of an oppressor who has been cruel to us remain around his neck forever, but they pass over us. (G:1-30)

꩜ Leader and the army exist to protect the people and prevent those responsible for abuses. If they do not protect the people, or worse if they abuse them, that leader does not deserve the title and his rule will not last. (A:92)

꩜ The leader must not take the suffering of the poor lightly. Ants in great numbers can paralyze a lion. Many mosquitoes can make a mighty elephant powerless. (A:141)

꩜ The sword of men is less effective than the cries of children and the pain of old women. (A:99)

꩜ Do good to others so that tomorrow God may not deal harshly with you. Be lenient with your underlings, for he may one day become the leader; like the pawn that becomes a queen. (B:2-4)

If the leader makes his followers suffer, they become the enemies of their own state. (A:52)

Leaders are only allowed pleasure and happiness if followers are assured peace and tranquility. They are like the shepherds who must protect their flock from the wolf. If they fail, they do not deserve any rewards. (A: 33)

When you build something on bad foundations, you destroy yourself. (A:98)

A leader's honor is not in new conquests, but in governing the state well. An ignorant man may be able to conquer the world, but can he keep it? (A:117)

If fate provokes the revenge of the weak and breaks the teeth of tyrants, it is only justice. (A:123)

If someone does not feel safe because of you, you should not feel safe around him. The snake attacks because it is afraid. Do not bring down a wall while standing under it; it will bury you. Do not kill the snake's young without fearing its attacks. That would not be wise. (A:83)

One who does not harm and hurt others, fears no one. The poisonous snake is afraid because it knows the harm it can do. The cat lives peacefully in the house because it knows it does not harm anyone and therefore no one will harm him. A wolf is never safe; it is always on guard because it does harm and he knows it. The beggars in the city are safe when they harm no one. The highway robbers are not because they are planning their evil deeds and they know it. (A:126)

~ It is a mistake to crush the fingers of a weak person with your powerful and strong arm. If you show no mercy to the fallen, don't be under the delusion that when you fall anyone will help you. Anyone who plants the seed of evil and expects to reap goodness is fantasizing in vain. (G:1-10)

The idea of accountability or karma is central to many religious and philosophical traditions. From that perspective, all human beings are answerable for their actions. For leaders, this accountability is even greater. The power and privilege that leaders have require that they be even more vigilant and responsible than others. Their power does not exempt them from blame; instead it intensifies their accountability. Leaders must take the responsibility of serving their followers seriously and act without reproach. If the reaction of their followers, and the basic duty to do good for goodness' sake are not enough to convince them, Saadi reminds them that they are answerable to higher authority. Their actions will catch up with them.

Afsaneh Nahavandi

Decisiveness (Ghate-iyat) and

Action-Orientation (Amal Garai)

"You must kill the wolf in the beginning, not after all the sheep have been killed."

The kindness and compassion of the leader must not be mistaken for indecision or weakness. The ideal leader is decisiveness and swift when necessary. Action is essential to leadership. Saadi does not recommend sitting back and letting events happen. His leaders are powerful and action-oriented. Leaders are responsible for addressing problems in a timely manner and not letting them fester. While leaders must be patient and cautious, they are expected to act when needed. Instead of action for the sake of action, leaders must be restrained but act swiftly and decisively when they have the needed knowledge and right opportunity.

❧ You must kill the wolf in the beginning, not after all the sheep have been killed. (A:33)

❧ Action, not words, is demanded by religion, for words without action are void of substance. (B:1-7)

❧ Beware of the fool who is as loud as ten men – a hundred arrows shot and all miss the target. If you are wise, shoot one, and make sure that one is straight. (B:7-2)

❧ Do not be soft when you should be harsh and firm. (A:147)

❧ Good leadership means thinking about tomorrow and not putting off what can be done today to tomorrow. (A: 88)

If someone commits a misdeed by error, it is better to first ignore it. If he repeats it, scare him. If he continues without remorse, destroy him. A bad seed can only give bad fruit. (A:107)

With strangers, a leader must show power. With friends, he must be kind. (A:61)

Do not let your enemy grow; do not let an enemy soldier find a horse. That is how chess is won. (A:134)

To punish an evildoer and leave him at his job is like catching a wolf and making him promise not to attack the sheep. (A:102)

If you see the beginning of serious trouble in someone, it is better to destroy him than exile him.

One does not chase away a snake by throwing him to a neighbor's house. (A:105)

When something comes out right without your interference, there is no point in speaking out. But if you see a blind man headed for a pit, it would be a sin to remain silent. (G:1-38)

Along with kindness and compassion, Saadi advocates strength and decisiveness. Remaining idle when leaders can take action to help others and address problems is not acceptable. Ideal leaders do not sit back to let events happen; they are proactive and practical. They must be careful and thoughtful, but they must decide and act. The power they are given obligates them to match their words with action and fulfill their duty as caretakers of their followers, organizations, or countries. The strong centralized, monarchic tradition of Persia is evident in Saadi's teachings. Kings are granted formidable power that they must use for the good of their followers.

Astuteness (Ziraki)

"Do good to those who wish you harm; it is better to keep a dog's mouth closed with a morsel."

Leaders' gracious, and compassionate approach and their integrity, fairness and action-orientation come with a healthy dose of astuteness, practicality, cunning and distrust. Effective leaders are aware of their surroundings, watchful of their enemies, advisors and followers, and keenly perceptive in regards to all that affects them and their followers. They are wise and prudent and clever enough to recognize and seek the path of least resistance to achieve their goals. While leaders must not sit idle, Saadi recommends that indirect action is often preferable and necessary. Leaders must be astute, shrewd and calculating to assure the wellbeing of their followers. However, in many cases, directly attacking powerful people can be foolish. In those cases, appeasement, patience, and deception are more likely to achieve goals. If leaders cannot achieve their goals by being passive and, more importantly, by setting up situations that lead to the desired results, they must then act with care and prudence.

While integrity is essential when dealing with followers, deception and cunning are allowed when fighting enemies. Deceit in military battles with the goal of defeating an enemy is as accepted in ancient Persian philosophy as it is in other cultures. However, deception cannot be used against followers or as means of advancing the leader's personal goals and ambitions. Effective leaders are like chess masters; they think strategically and set up situations that lead to success. However, even in dealing with enemies, Saadi recommends shunning cruelty and trying to win them over with kindness when possible.

~&> Do good to those who wish you harm; it is better to keep a dog's mouth closed with a morsel. (G:1-33)

~&> Set up one of your enemies against another. No matter which one wins, you are victorious. (A:133)

~&> Give a delicate mission to two people who don't get along. This will prevent them from agreeing to betray you. If the wolves fight, the sheep are safe. (A:62)

❧ If an enemy can be bought, it is better not to use violence because blood is worth much more than gold. (A:90)

❧ Be courteous and do good with friends and enemies. Your friends will love you more and your enemies will hate you less. (A:36)

❧ O friend! Be humble when you are dealing with a fierce foe, for gentleness will blunt the sharpest sword. (B:4-15)

❧ Quote writers and poets from time to time in public. If they have written something inappropriate, it will be revealed. (A:59)

❧ If you are going to forgive someone, arrange for powerful people to ask you to do so. You will then have a reason to pardon. (A:70)

❧ One good rule of leadership is to avoid confronting strong people. This would not be reasonable. One must not act against weaker people either; that would be unworthy. (A:72)

❧ You cannot vanquish your enemies if they are united. You can only win if you develop a friendship with some of them. (A:132)

❧ When you are not in need, build friendships. They will serve you when you are in need. (A:135)

❧ An intelligent person will submit to an unworthy person who is enjoying good fortune and has power. If you don't have a sharp claw, it would be better not to tangle with wild beasts. Anyone who wrestles with someone with a steely arm will only hurt his own poor hand. Wait until fate ties his hands, and then rip out his brains to the delight of your friends. (G1-21)

﹏ If you want peace with your enemy, praise him to his face every time he speaks ill of you behind your back. A mean person's words come out of his mouth; if you don't want him to be bitter, make his mouth sweet. (G:1-24)

The recommendation for astuteness, shrewdness, and even cunning is as much part of Saadi's teachings as his advocacy of integrity, kindness and moderation. The intelligent leader is a strategic thinker who carefully considers consequences of his or her actions and uses all possible actions to get the desired results with as little disruption as possible. In some cases, inaction is advisable; in others, deception and force can be used with enemies when all other options are eliminated. The astuteness goes hand in hand with action-orientation. Leaders are responsible for the welfare of their followers. To that end, they must be smart, perceptive, and practical and take the best course of action.

LEADERS IMPLICATONS
FOR TODAY'S

Leadership and its many challenges continue to draw our attention. People hope for good leadership that will move them towards goals effectively and take care of their needs as individuals. They also yearn for leadership that can transform their organization, community, or country for the better and help build a prosperous future for their children. We indeed have high expectations of our leaders. We learn early in life, through stories, that leaders – king, queens, and princes in fairy tales – impact us. They can contribute to our happiness if they are good and just or bring us misery if they are evil and capricious. As adults, we follow the actions of political and business leaders. The popular media also turns entertainers and sports figures into role models who are directly or indirectly assigned leadership status. Leaders matter; we seek good leadership to guide us out of social, political, organizational, and community turmoil.

Years of research in leadership have taught us much about what makes good and bad leadership and what aspiring leaders should do. Saadi's lessons are in full agreement with the findings of modern leadership research. They also echo the insight that results from the intuition and experience of practiced and effective leaders. His teachings are direct, practical and simple and carry the wisdom of thousands of years of practice and tradition. As a sage and philosopher, his teachings are further informed by his extensive and lengthy travels, the many hardships he endured, the insight he acquired through his interactions with wise mentors and teachers, and his keen observations of the human condition. He wrote his books in the twilight years of his life, after he returned home from many years of wandering and encountering people from many walks of life, cultures, and religions. His words of wisdom are rooted in an ancient civilization that ruled the world, underwent unspeakable destruction and had, even by the 13th century, already made extensive contributions to science, literature, and the world's cultural heritage. The leaders Saadi observed and wrote about – both good and bad – were tested in more dire circumstances than what most of us will experience. They succeeded and failed through crisis and turmoil. We can benefit from their experience and wisdom and there is much Saadi can offer us.

The principles presented by Saadi are based on duty, honor, compassion, accountability and responsibility without selfishness, greed and personal ambition. Some may argue that such ideals are archaic and outdated; leadership is not about caring and compassion. Instead, some would say, it is all about innovation and boldness, quick action and pushing the envelope in all areas. Some would contend that bold and innovative leaders are necessarily arrogant and ambitious, that they require individual recognition, and sometimes have to sacrifice established principles and individual consideration on the road to success. Indeed, many of today's celebrated organizational and political leaders would provide excellent examples of this philosophy. However, progress and success do not require trampling people or principles and do not necessitate arrogance and blind ambition. While innovation and boldness are as essential today as they have been in the past, they do not conflict with duty, honor, compassion, accountability and responsibility that are principles that make a society civil and allow us to prosper and live in peace. These principles provide the indispensable order, predictability, organization, and accountability that allow individuals, communities and societies to thrive. They are what make us human and allow us to aspire to be the best that we can be. A leader who practices these principles will create an environment where followers, along with the leader, dedicate themselves to one another's wellbeing, are bold and look for solutions to problems, innovate, and address problems cooperatively without sacrificing integrity, kindness, humility, and prudence.

Leadership, no matter the setting, is about service to others. It is not and should not be about fulfilling the leader's personal ambitions, making him or her look good, more powerful, or wealthier, or about getting so far ahead of followers that they no longer follow you or even know where their leader is. Leadership is also about making decisions, taking action when necessary, being responsible for the community, organization, or state and being accountable for one's actions. These are not for the faint-hearted. They are challenging and as a result come with considerable power and privilege that must be used to advance the common goals. The same power and privilege however, have the potential to go to the leaders' head or at worst make them corrupt and abusive. Therefore, staying humble and connected to followers and being well grounded are probably among the biggest challenges of leadership, especially leadership at high levels.

Putting Saadi's Principles into Practice

Have unwavering integrity. Integrity counts. It is not culture or situation specific; it matters to followers everywhere. "Walking the talk," being honest and truthful, and guarding one's reputation are essential to a leader's ability to be effective. Followers demand it and deserve it. No one trusts and follows – at least not willingly and not for long – a leader who lies and cheats. Act and speak with integrity and authenticity and carefully build and guard your reputation as a truthful and trustworthy leader.

Have integrity in all that you do and guard your reputation. It is a simple choice!

Be kind. As a follower, most of us expect some degree of kindness and compassion from our leader. These are not words that are readily associated with leadership; action and decisiveness – yes, compassion – less likely. Many political and business leaders disregard the importance of kindness and compassion and argue that their job is to get things done, not take care of people. They will content that they are not parents; they are organizational or national leaders. Saadi is telling us differently. Kindness and compassion are essential and necessary to good leadership. *Leadership is not about things; it's about people.* To engage people and motivate them and encourage them to give their best, you must care about them. Without caring about your followers, nothing can get done, or at least nothing can get done well. Treat others well and treat them equitably and without bias. As is the case with integrity, this should not be a difficult choice. Being kind, compassionate, and forgiving do not make you weak; it makes you a stronger and better leader. It does not stop you from moving forward and getting things done; it makes it easier to achieve your goals. In today's highly competitive, materialistic and cutthroat environment, it may be challenging to remain kind and compassionate. However, being human means taking care of others; it is a basic tenet of every religion and every civil society and should be a guide to everyone's behavior. It is also a particular responsibility of those in leadership roles.

Take care of your followers; be kind and compassionate when it's easy and be kind and compassionate even when it's hard. It will pay off for you and for your organization.

Be humble. Leadership is about others; it is about service. It is not and should not be about glorifying the leader. Saadi, and many modern leadership theorists, believe that leaders are servants. Leadership comes with power. The higher the leader's position, the more his or her power and the easier it is to become isolated, and imperious. Power can be heady. One of the major challenges leaders face is to remain humble and unpretentious when given power, privilege, rewards, and recognition. The arrogant leaders who show hubris and act with a sense of self-importance and impunity do not start out that way; they acquire those behaviors as they gain power. Followers play a key role in this process by glorifying leaders. Being entrusted with a leadership position is a privilege and an opportunity that must be accepted with humility and used for the betterment of others. Focus on remaining humble and surround yourself with courageous advisors and followers who will speak truth to power and help you remain grounded.

Focus on serving your followers and remind yourself that your power comes from them, not the other way around.

Take the middle road. Extremes are enticing and may be exhilarating. We live in times when extremes are sought out and valued. Many hunger for increasing stimulation that comes from engaging in thrilling activities that start an unending cycle. Taking extreme risks, for potentially high rewards is becoming the norm and celebrated in western popular culture. Leadership is not immune from this trend. However, ancient wisdom from many cultures and philosophical approaches advocate the middle road – the Golden Mean – instead. Saadi recommends moderation in all things. Nothing done to the extreme is healthy and productive in the long run. When you have responsibility for others' life and welfare, as leaders do, taking moderate actions becomes even more essential. Being on the extremes can endanger not only your own livelihood, but also that of your followers. The path of moderation does not shun innovation and creativity; it simply advocates careful and thoughtful action that is most likely to benefit the largest number of people.

Unless there is a crisis, take the middle course and shun the extremes.

Be cautious. Leaders are responsible for other people's lives, either directly or indirectly. They are role models for their followers. Their actions are observed and imitated and these actions have consequences. Because leaders affect so many others around them, it behooves them to be prudent in their actions and decisions. You must watch your own behavior and be careful in your decisions. The kindness and compassion that Saadi advocates comes with a healthy dose of skepticism and vigilance to avoid being duped and preventing those around the leader from taking advantage of him or her and their position.

Be careful in your actions and farsighted in your decisions. Consider the long-term consequences of what you say and do.

Consult with experts. More than ever, leaders are facing highly intricate situations that demand diverse and deep expertise. No one person, no matter how intelligent, intuitive, or experienced, knows everything. Saadi's advice to seek the help of wise people with knowledge and experience rings even more true in today's world where the amount and complexity of information have increased exponentially. Modern leadership theory and research also strongly suggest that leaders consult others, particularly in complex situations and when they need their followers' support. Whether you follow Saadi's advice or the modern research findings, consult with people who have expertise. Action, innovation, and creativity are not the sole responsibility of the leaders. Followers are the most significant source of ideas, innovation, and productivity. Furthermore, even when innovation is critical, having the right experience matters. Saadi places considerable emphasis on the power of wisdom that comes from experience and age. Neither is highly valued in today's youth-oriented culture. Instead, we tend to focus on the newest and flashiest ideas or people, without fully considering their ability to deliver an actual outcome. The disregard for experience often means that we ignore the past and make unnecessary and avoidable mistakes.

Do not lead alone! Get help from experts and rely on others' experience and wisdom.

Be accountable. The power and privilege that come with leadership demand accountability to followers, and to higher authority. Leaders must accept responsibility for their actions, successes, and failures.

Power does not allow leaders to act with impunity. If anything, they are held to higher standards than their followers. While followers are allowed mistakes and should be forgiven when they are committed in good faith, leaders do not have such a luxury. As role models, they have little room for error.'

Accept responsibility for your actions and decisions and hold yourself accountable for your own and your followers' actions.

Be decisive. In case Saadi's teachings appear to advocate a lenient and indulgent leader who is focused on pleasing followers without making difficult decisions, keep in mind that he strongly advocates action. Leaders must make decisions and act when necessary. They must not act in haste and simply for the sake of doing something. They must be careful and judicious in their actions, but they must act; words alone are not enough. They must use all that is available to them to achieve their goals and protect their followers.

Talk alone is not enough. Be decisive and act when necessary.

Be astute. Leaders must be aware of their environment and clever and shrewd about their actions. Kindness and compassion do not exclude astuteness. The effective leader is a chess master who carefully considers his or her actions, executes plans thoughtfully, and is keenly aware of the consequences of his or her actions. Doing nothing or using deception may be appropriate courses of action, but only when they are conscious choices and part of a long-term strategy.

Think like a chess master. Think long-term and use all that you can to benefit your followers.

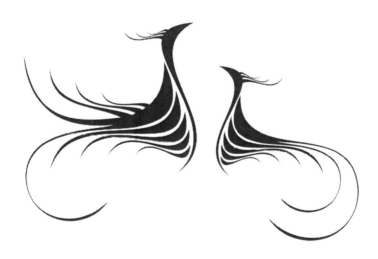

CPSIA information can be obtained at www.ICGtesting.com
Printed in the USA
BVOW040259270412

288763BV00003B/1/P